EUROPA
(Earth's Cry Heaven's Smile)

Music by
CARLOS SANTANA
and TOM COSTER

Europa - 5 - 1

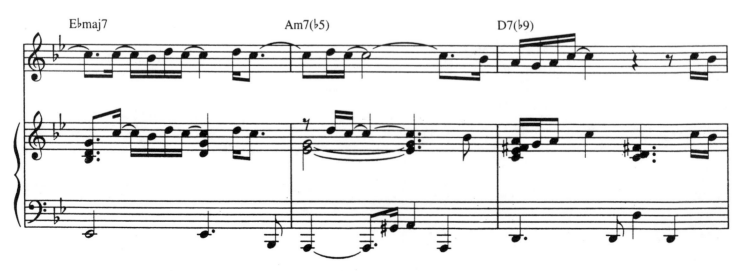

Love Songs for Lovers

A Collection of Romantic Songs

9102A

Project Manager: Zobeida Pérez
Cover Design: María A. Chenique

Contents

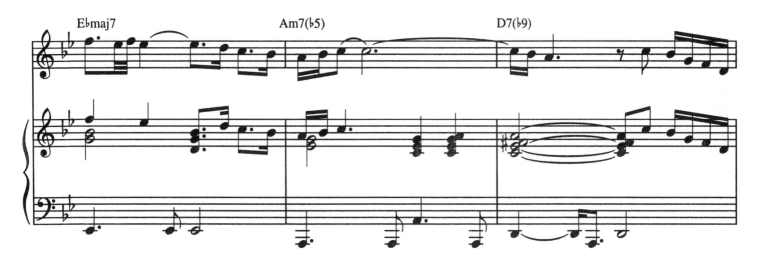

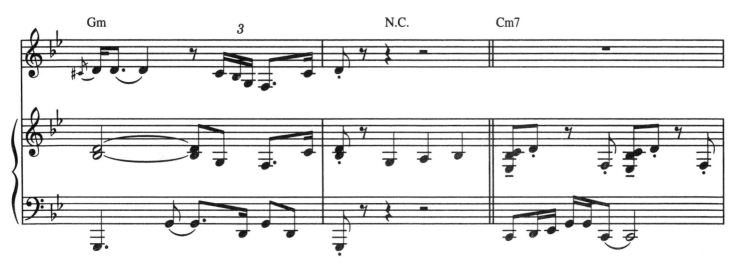

6

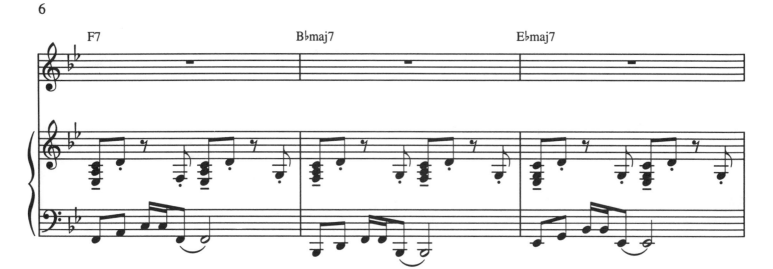

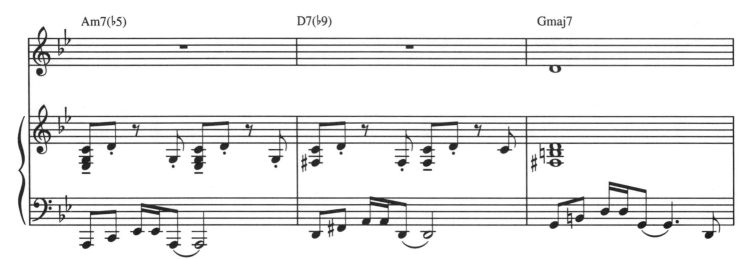

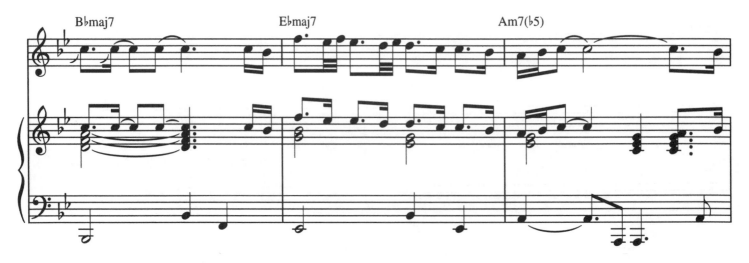

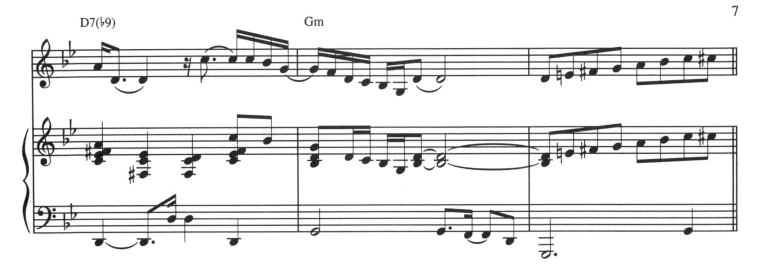

Repeat ad lib. & fade

FEEL LIKE MAKIN' LOVE

Words and Music by
EUGENE McDANIELS

DO THAT TO ME ONE MORE TIME

Words and Music by
TONI TENNILLE

Do That to Me One More Time - 4 - 1

CAN I TOUCH YOU. . . THERE?

Words and Music by
MICHAEL BOLTON, ROBERT JOHN "MUTT" LANGE,
BERNARD EDWARDS and NILE RODGERS

%. **Dm7** *Bridge:*

Clos-er, ba - by, clos - er, come on, let's_ be - gin._ Ooh, love is tak - in' o - ver,___
Clos-er, ba - by, clos - er, can't be close_ e - nough._ I can't help the way_ I hold_ you, I just
— *(Instrumental solo ad lib....*

got to let___ it in._____ } Ooh,_____ and I need to feel__ the heart_
hun - ger for___ your love._____ } ...end solo)
...end solo)

___ of you._ I need to reach_ the ver - y deep - est part___ of you._

Chorus:

All I wan-na do____

____ is touch____ you ba - by, touch the ver - y soul____ in - side____ of you.____

Let me be____ the one____ to show____ you just what love____ can do._____

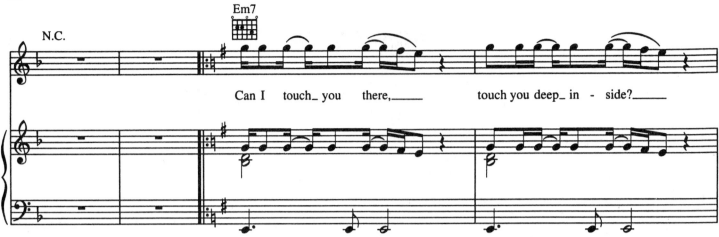

Can I touch_ you there,_____ touch you deep_ in - side?_____

Can I touch_ your heart,_____ the way___ you're touch - in' mine?_____ Can I touch_

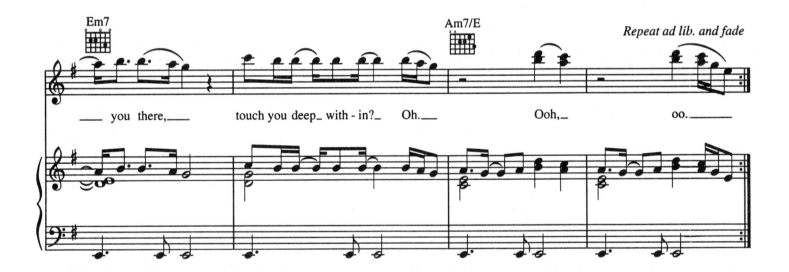

___ you there,___ touch you deep_ with - in?_ Oh.___ Ooh,_ oo._____

BREATHE

Words and Music by
HOLLY LAMAR and STEPHANIE BENTLEY

Slowly ♩ = 60

mp

(with pedal)

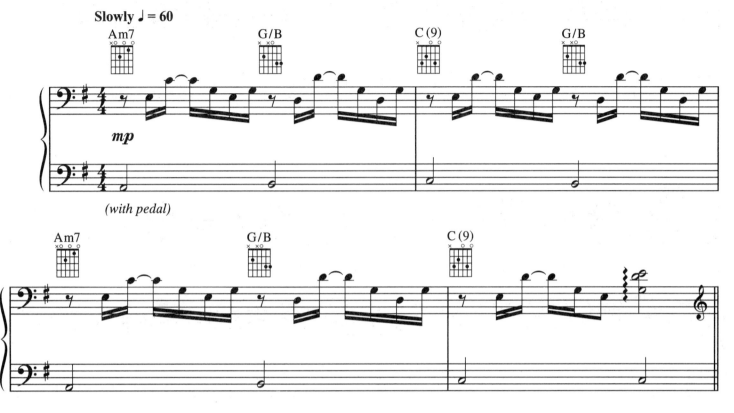

Verse 1:

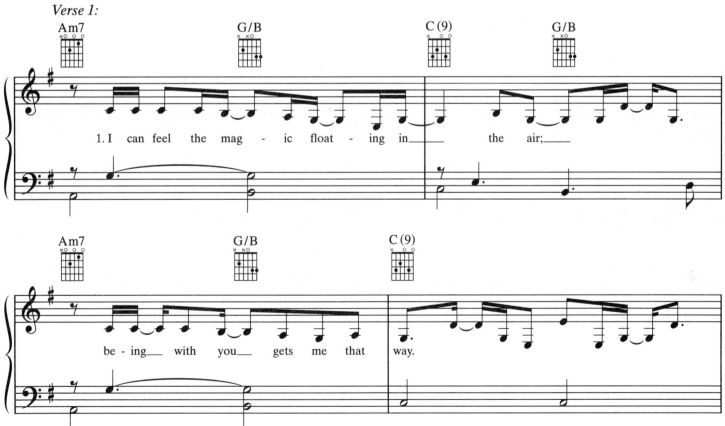

1. I can feel the mag - ic float - ing in the air;

be - ing with you gets me that way.

Breathe - 5 - 1

hear is the beat-ing of____ your heart.

there's no need for words_ right now.__

cresc. *mf*

'Cause I can feel you

Chorus:

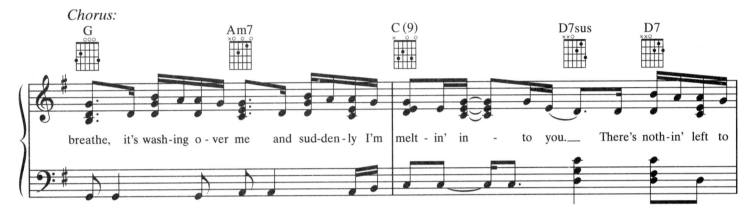

breathe, it's wash-ing o - ver me and sud-den-ly I'm melt - in' in - to you._ There's noth-in' left to

prove, ba - by, all we need is just_ to be_ caught_ up in the

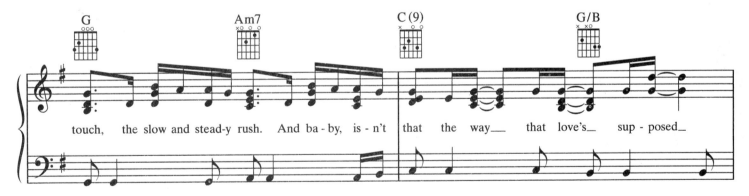

touch, the slow and stead-y rush. And ba - by, is - n't that the way_ that love's_ sup - posed_

to be? *dim.* *mp* I can feel you

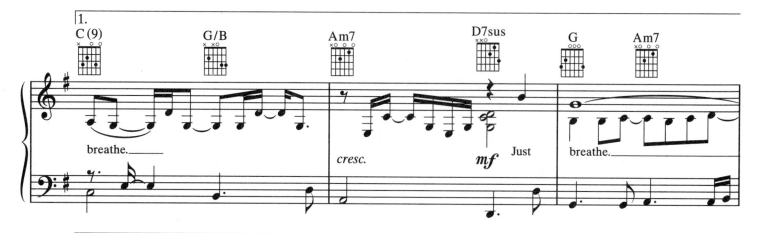

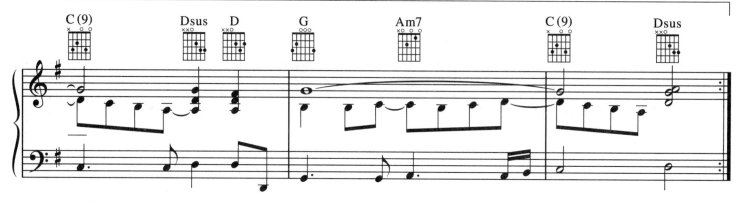

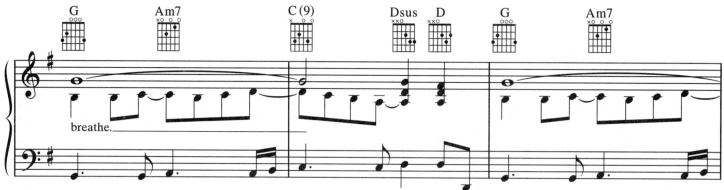

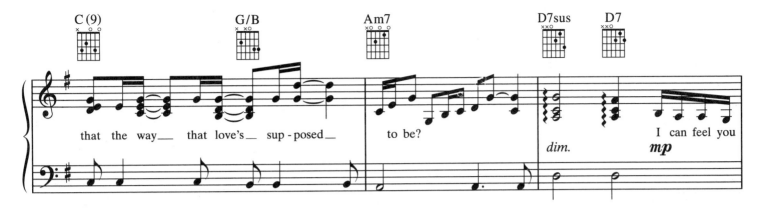

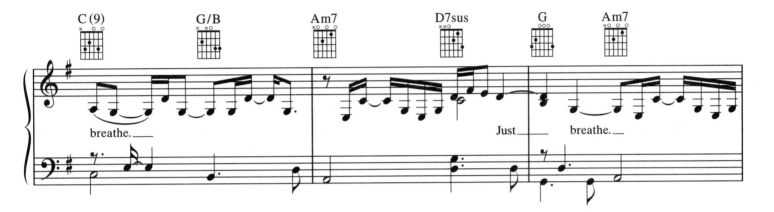

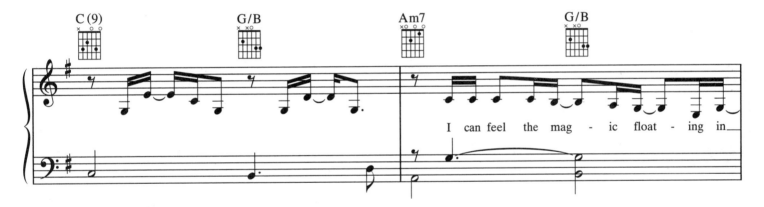

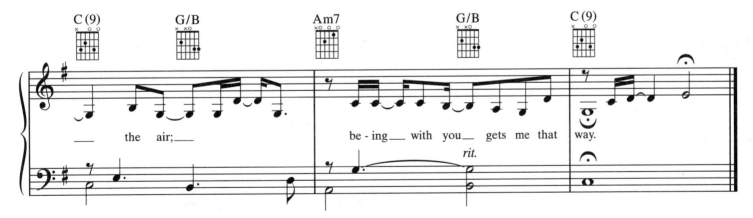

BY THE TIME THIS NIGHT IS OVER

Words and Music by
MICHAEL BOLTON, ANDY GOLDMARK
and DIANE WARREN

By the Time This Night Is Over - 6 - 1

closer and closer and closer, by the time this night is

1. o - ver. —

2. o - ver. —

A night like this may

nev - er come a - gain.___ And you won't want this night to end.___

LOVE TO LOVE YOU, BABY

Words and Music by
PETE BELLOTTE, GIORGIO MORODER
and DONNA SUMMER

Love to Love You, Baby - 3 - 1

LOVE WON'T LET ME WAIT

Words and Music by
VINNIE BARRETT and BOBBY ELI

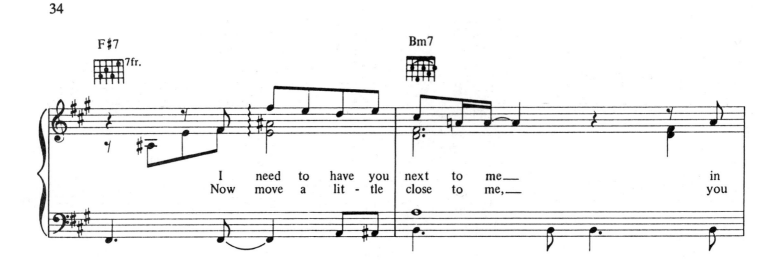

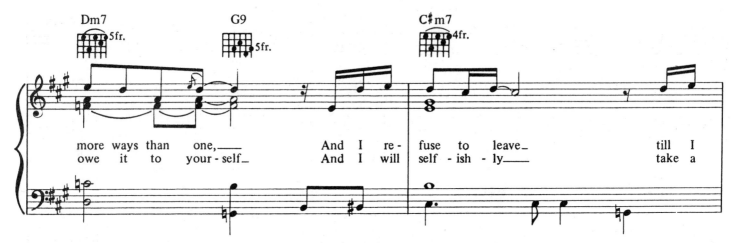

BETCHA BY GOLLY WOW

Words and Music by
THOM BELL and LINDA CREED

Moderately slow

Betcha by Golly Wow - 4 - 1

ev - er, — And ev - er will my love for you keep grow - ing strong, keep

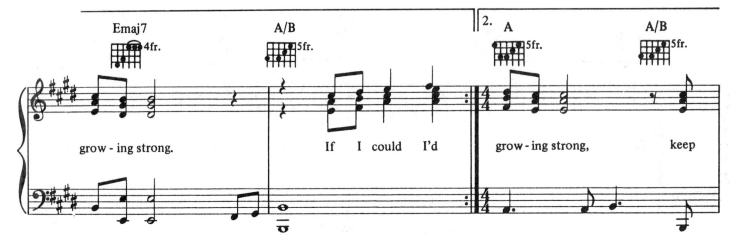

grow - ing strong. If I could I'd grow - ing strong, keep

grow - ing strong.

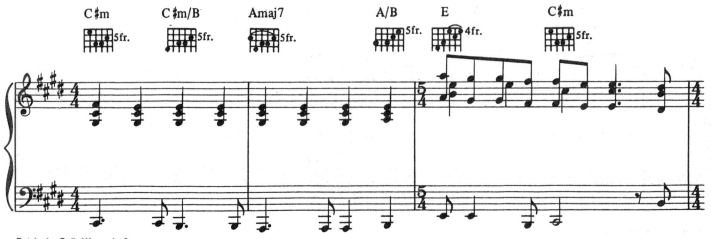

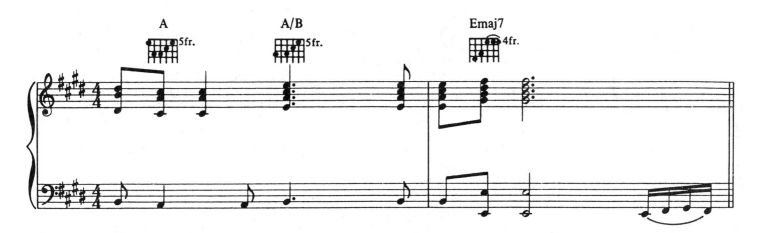

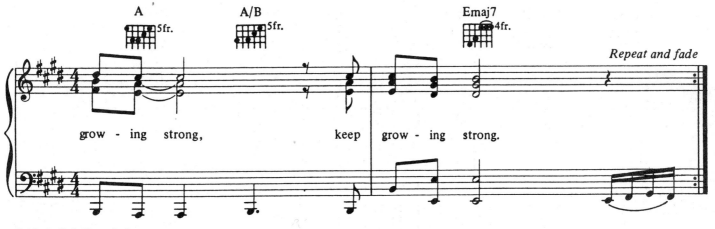

Betcha by Golly Wow - 4 - 4

2 BECOME 1

Words and Music by
SPICE GIRLS, MATTHEW ROWEBOTTOM
and RICHARD STANNARD

2 Become 1 - 5 - 1

be for real—don't be— a stran-ger. We can a-chieve—it, we can a-chieve— it._____

—— Come a lit-tle bit clo-ser ba-by,—— get it on, get it on,—— 'cause to-night——

—— is the night—— when two be-come one.—— I

need some love like I nev-er need-ed love be-fore,— (wan-na make love to ya ba-by.) I

had a lit-tle love now I'm back for more, (wan-na make love to ya ba-by.)

Set your spi-rit free,— it's the on-ly way— to be._____

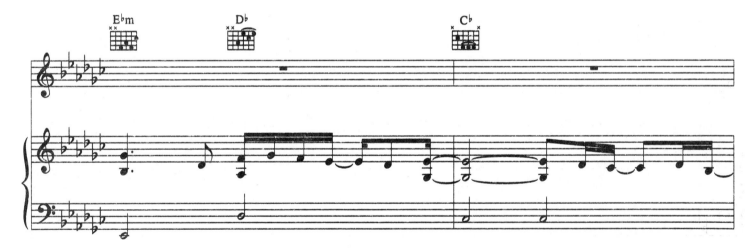

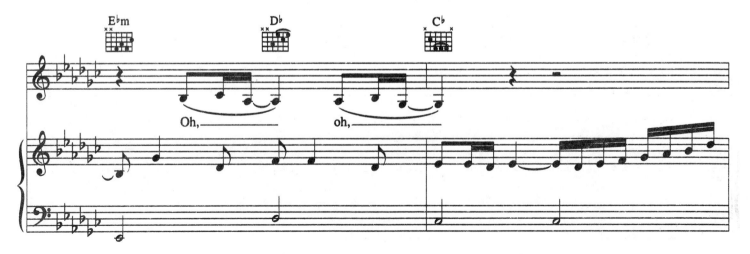

Oh,_____ oh,_____

be a lit-tle bit wis-er ba-by,___ put it on, put it on,___ 'cause to-night___

___ is the night___ when two be-come one.___ I

need some love like I nev-er need-ed love be-fore,___ (wan-na make love to ya ba-by.) I

had a lit-tle love, now I'm back for more, (wan-na make love to ya ba-by.) I

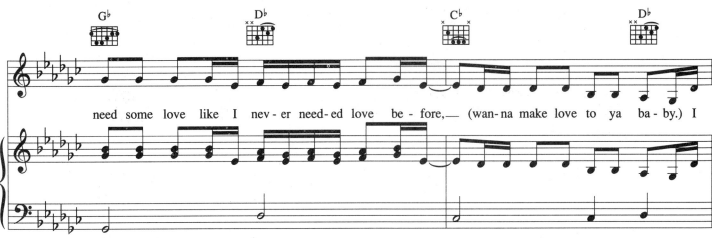

need some love like I nev-er need-ed love be-fore,— (wan-na make love to ya ba-by.) I

had a lit-tle love, now I'm back for more, (wan-na make love to ya ba-by.)

Repeat to fade

Set your spi-rit free,— it's the on-ly way to be.— It's the

Verse 2:
Silly games that you were playing, empty words we both were saying,
Let's work it out boy, let's work it out boy.
Any deal that we endeavour, boys and girls feel good together,
Take it or leave it, take it or leave it.
Are you as good as I remember baby, get it on, get it on,
'Cause tonight is the night when two become one.

I need some love like I never needed love before, (wanna make love to ya baby.)
I had a little love, now I'm back for more, (wanna make love to ya baby.)
Set your spirit free, it's the only way to be.

HOLD ME (IN YOUR ARMS)

Words and Music by
MICHAEL MASSER and
LINDA CREED

Chorus:

arms to - night, __ fill __ my life __

with plea - sure. Let's not waste this

pre - cious time, __ this mo - ment's ours to

trea - sure. Hold me in your arms to - night, __

and make it last ___ for - ev - er. ___

When the morn - ing sun ap - pears _

we'll find our ___ way to - geth - er. ___

Verse 2:

(Girl:) I believe you, when you say that you love me;
Know that I won't take you for granted.
Tonight the magic has begun.
So won't you hold me, touch me,
Make me your woman tonight?

(Boy:) There's something in your eyes I see
I won't betray your trust in me.

(I Wanna Take) FOREVER TONIGHT

Words and Music by
ANDY GOLDMARK
and ERIC CARMEN

1. Feel your breath_

Verse:

_ on my shoul- der, and I know we could-n't get an- y clos-
_ I'm on fi- re, you're the on- ly one I'll ev- er de- sire._

I don't wan - na act tough,__ I just wan - na fall in love.__ As we move__
Turn the light down low,__ make the world go slow.__ When I'm hold -

__ in - to the night, I get cra - zy think-ing
- ing you to - night, it's so ea - sy. Noth-ing

how it's gon - na be with you ba - by. I don't wan - na play__ rough,__ I've been lov -
moves me like you do when you tease__ me. And to rush would be a crime,__ I just wan -

ing you e - nough,__ oh,__ ba - by.__ I wan - na take for -
na spend some time__ with you ba - by.__

Chorus:

ev - er to - night,___ wan - na stay___ in this mo - ment for - ev -

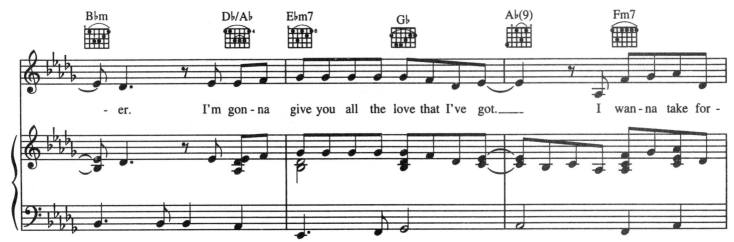

- er. I'm gon - na give you all the love that I've got.___ I wan - na take for -

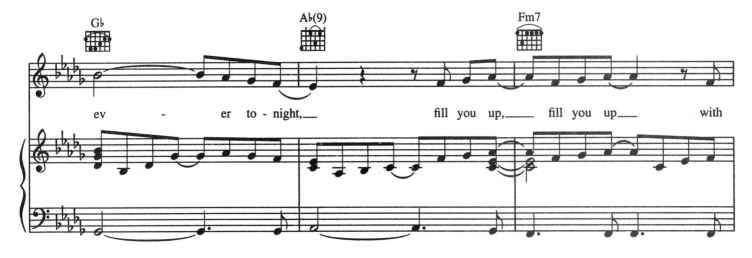

ev - er to - night,___ fill you up,___ fill you up___ with

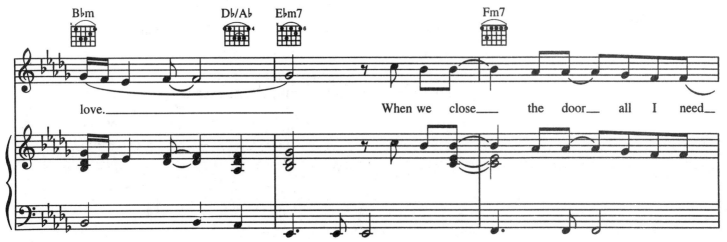

love._____ When we close___ the door___ all I need___

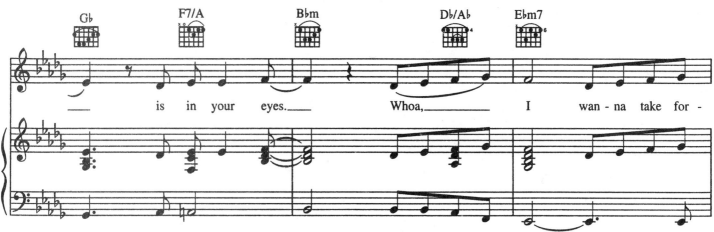

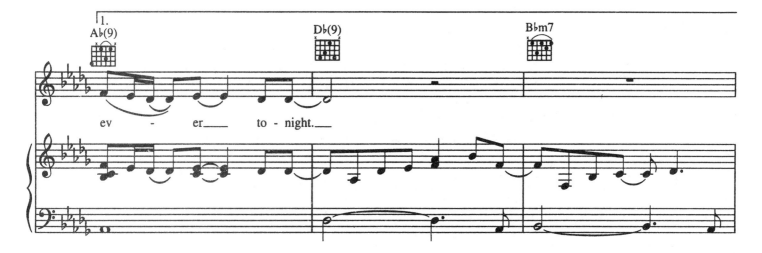

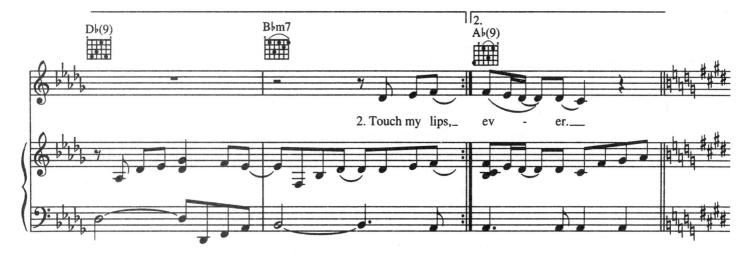

Oh,__ ba - by, I nev-er want to leave, I on-ly wan-na be with you,____ 'cause I

love how you feel,_ your love is so real._ I on - ly know I wan-na take for -

Chorus:

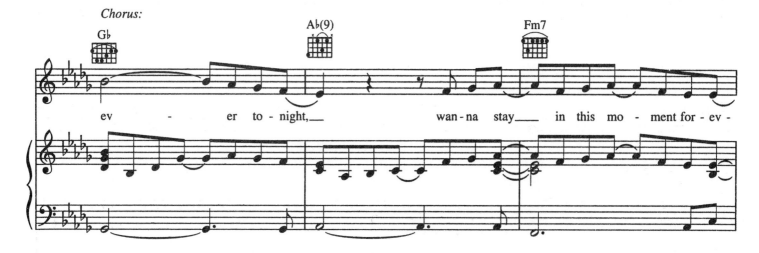

ev - er to - night,__ wan - na stay__ in this mo - ment for - ev -

- er. I'm gon - na give you all the love that I've got.__ I wan - na take for -

ev - er to - night,___ wan - na stay___ in this mo - ment for - ev -

- er. I'm gon - na give you all the love that I've got.___ 'Cause I can't live with - out___

___ you.

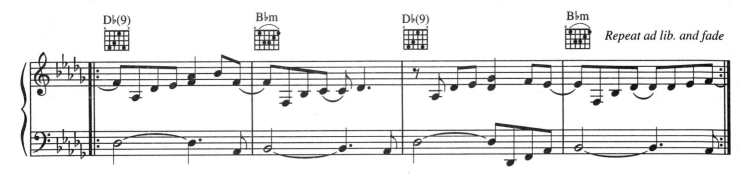

Repeat ad lib. and fade

I CAN'T WAIT ANOTHER MINUTE

Words and Music by
ERIC FOSTER WHITE

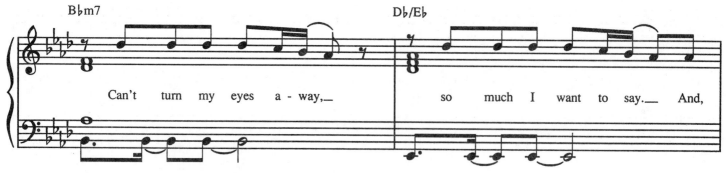

I Can't Wait Another Minute - 5 - 1

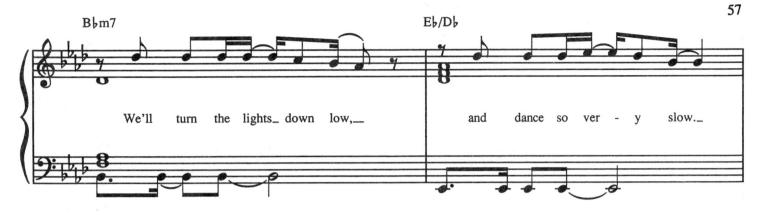

We'll turn the lights_ down low,_ and dance so ver - y slow._

I know that we don't know each oth - er well,_ but I

can't be - lieve_ I'm wast - ing your time,_ oh_ no._

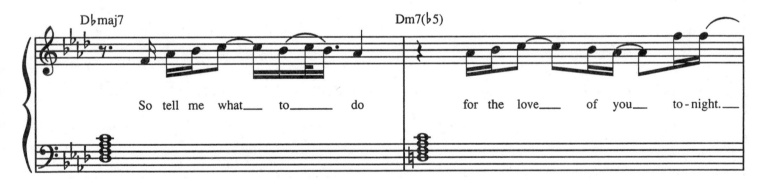

So tell me what_ to_ do for the love_ of you_ to - night._

'Cause I've been hold - ing back what_ I feel, love's so

real,___ But I can't wait an-oth-er min-ute, I can't

wait an-oth-er min-ute. 'Cause I've been hold-ing back all___ I feel, I'm for

real,___ 'cause I can't wait an-oth-er min-ute, I can't

wait an-oth-er min-ute for___ your love.___ Your_ love._

Ooh ooh ooh_ ooh ooh___ ooh._ Nuh,___ help_ now_ ba-by.___

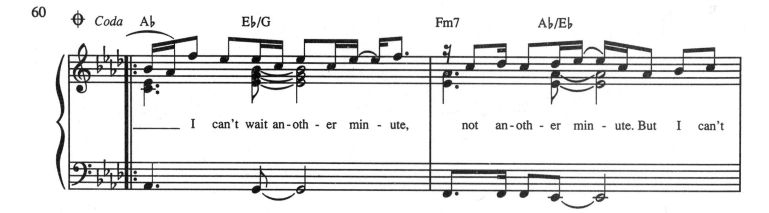

I can't wait an-oth-er min-ute, not an-oth-er min-ute. But I can't

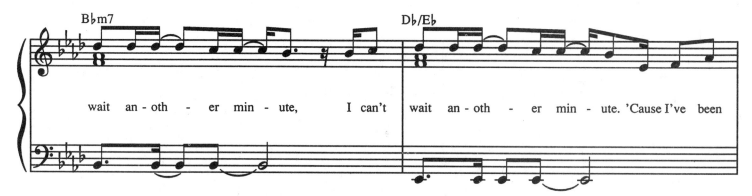

wait an-oth-er min-ute, I can't wait an-oth-er min-ute. 'Cause I've been

hold-ing back all___ I feel, I'm for real.___ 'Cause I can't

Repeat ad lib. and fade

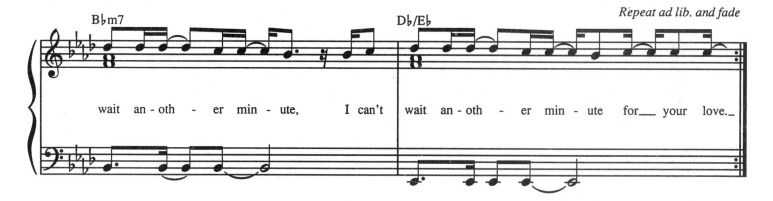

wait an-oth-er min-ute, I can't wait an-oth-er min-ute for___ your love.___

Verse 2:
Sweet lady, don't you look away.
I don't mean to make you shy,
But we haven't got much time.
Tonight, I know just what to say.
I'll love your cares away; you and I will find a way.
You know that there's a possibility
That we'll never get this chance once again.
So tell me what to do for the love of you tonight.
(To Chorus:)

JUST BECAUSE

Words and Music by
MICHAEL O'HARA, ALEX BROWN
and SAMI McKINNEY

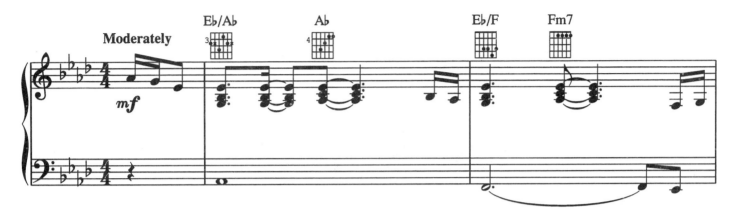

Oo. _____

Oo. _____ Ah. ____

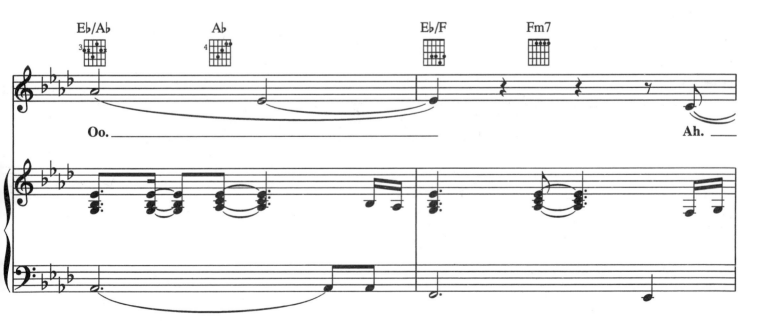

Just Because - 7 - 1

When I

think a - bout _ how much I'm lov - ing you, no lim - i -
dia - mond in _ my mind, a trea - sure found, a pre - cious

ta - tions, no set of reg - i - men - ted rules, _ I'm a
gem to me, _ you're so nice to have _ a - round. _ I'm so

mazed how much this love has touched _ my life, _ and the com -
glad I took the path that led _ to this. _ And it's a -

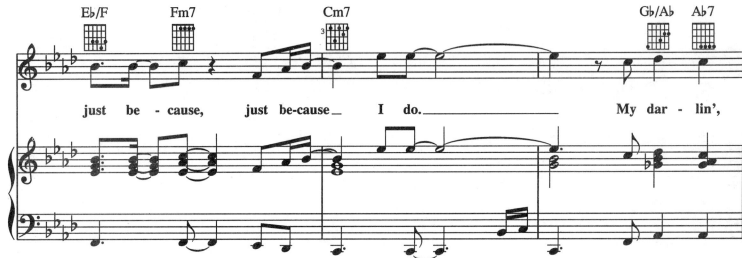

I'M IN THE MOOD FOR LOVE

Words and Music by
JIMMY McHUGH and
DOROTHY FIELDS

I'm In The Mood For Love — Sim-ply be-cause you're near me — Fun-ny, but when you're near me — I'm In The Mood For Love. — Heav-en is in your eyes — Bright as the stars we're un-der — Oh! Is it an-y won-der

I'm in the Mood for Love - 2 - 1

MOONDANCE

Words and Music by
VAN MORRISON

73

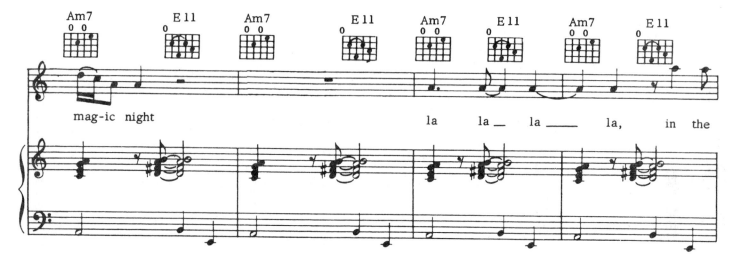

Moondance - 4 - 4

LADY

Words and Music by
LIONEL RICHIE

* Recorded 1/2 step higher, in E♭ minor

Lady - 4 - 1

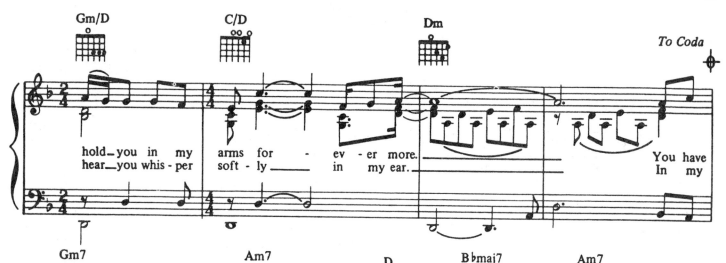

Lady - 4 - 2

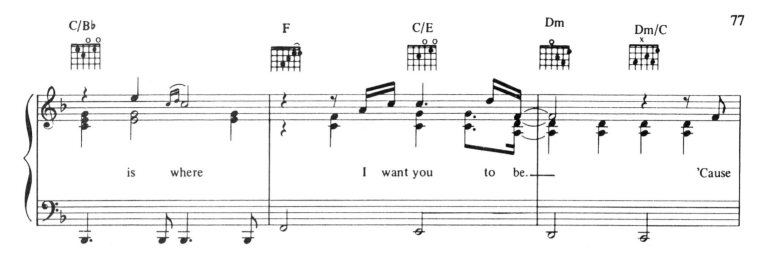

is where   I want you   to be.____   'Cause

my love,____   there's some-thing   I ____ want you ____ to

know.   You're the love____ of my life,____   you're my

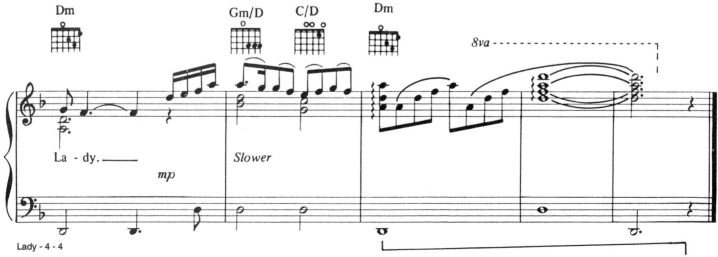

La - dy.____   *Slower*   you're my

mp

LOVE COME DOWN

Words and Music by
KASHIF

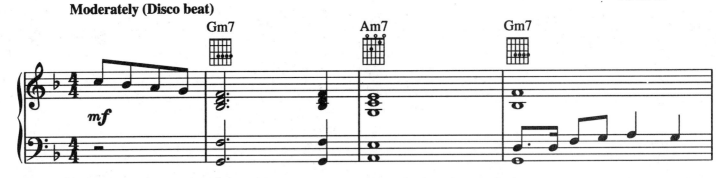

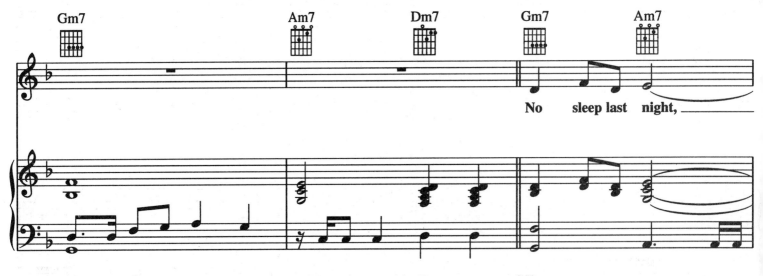

Love Come Down - 4 - 1

(YOU DRIVE ME) CRAZY

Words and Music by JÖRGEN ELOFSSON,
DAVID KREUGER, PER MAGNUSSON and MAX MARTIN

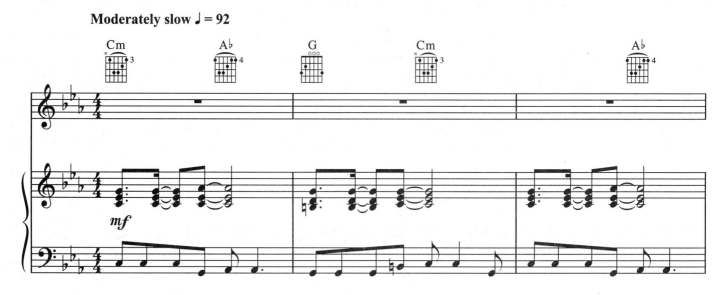

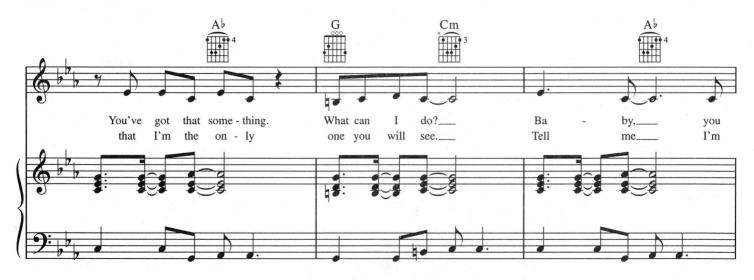

(You Drive Me) Crazy - 5 - 1

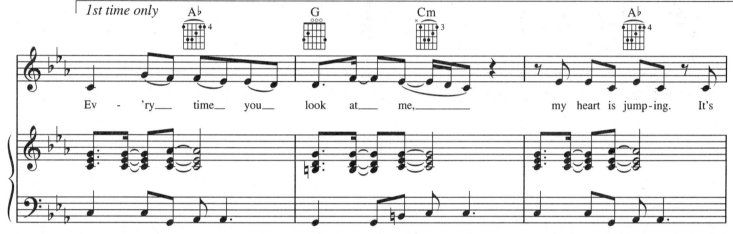

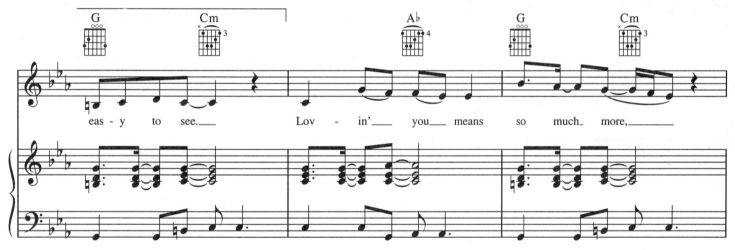

Bridge:

Craz-zy,_____ I just can't_____ sleep._____ I'm so ex-cit-ed, I'm in too_ deep._____ Cra-zy,_____ but it feels al - right._____ Ev - 'ry day and ev - 'ry night._____ You drive me

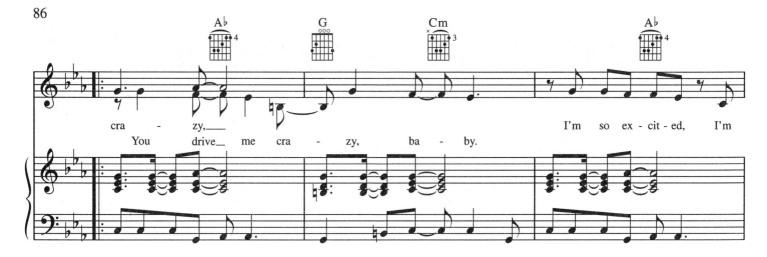

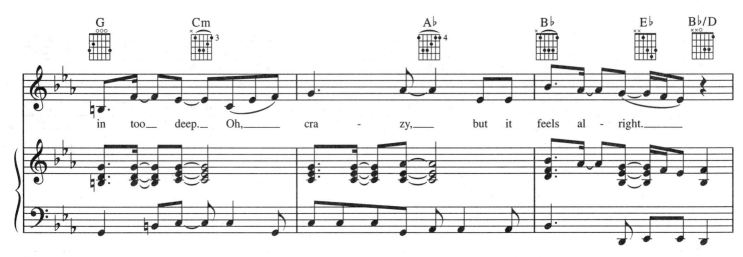

CAN'T FIGHT THE MOONLIGHT
(Theme from Coyote Ugly)

Words and Music by
DIANE WARREN

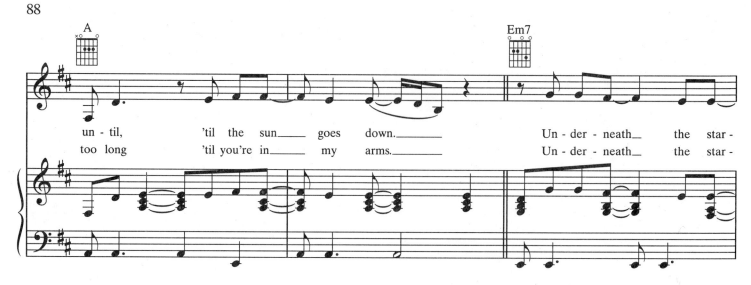

un - til, 'til the sun___ goes down._____ Un - der - neath__ the star-
too long 'til you're in___ my arms._____ Un - der - neath__ the star-

light, star - light,___ there's a mag - i - cal feel - ing so___ right.
light, star - light,___ we'll be lost__ in a rhy - thm so___ right.

Chorus:

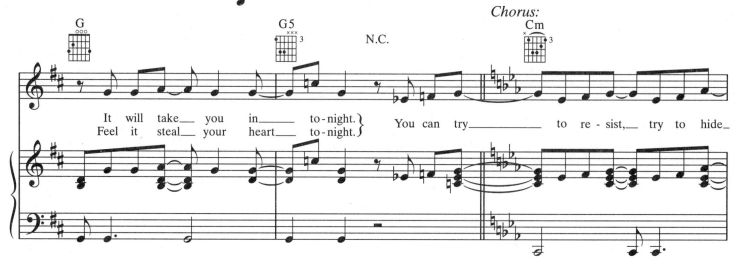

It will take__ you in___ to - night.⎱
Feel it steal__ your heart___ to - night.⎰ You can try_____ to re - sist,__ try to hide_

__ from my kiss,__ but you know,__ but you know__ that you can't fight the moon - light. Deep_

in the dark,___ you'll sur-ren-der your heart.___ Don't you know,___

___ don't you know___ that you can't fight the moon-light, no,___ you can't fight

1. it. It's gon-na get to your heart.___ 2. it.

No mat-ter what you do the night is gon-na get to you.___

90

Bridge:

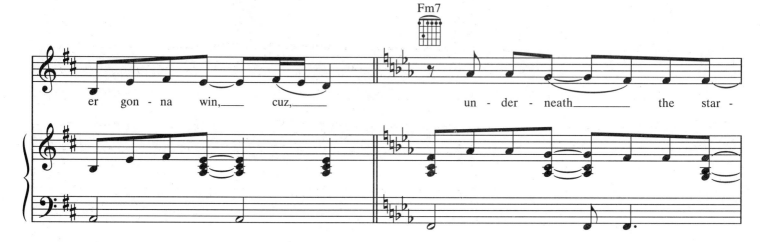

From the United Artists Motion Picture "THE SPY WHO LOVED ME"

NOBODY DOES IT BETTER

Lyrics by
CAROLE BAYER SAGER
Slowly

Music by
MARVIN HAMLISCH

Nobody Does It Better - 3 - 1

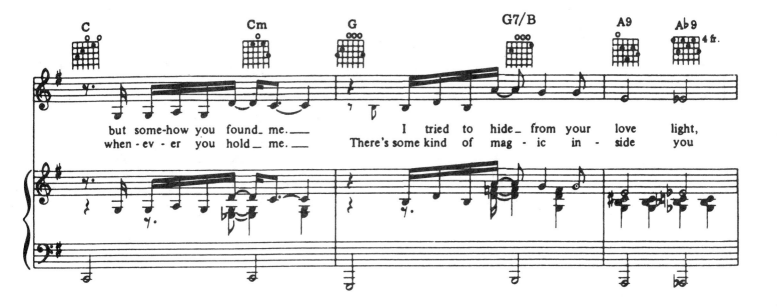

but some-how you found__ me.__ I tried to hide__ from your love light,
when-ev - er you hold__ me.__ There's some kind of mag - ic in - side you

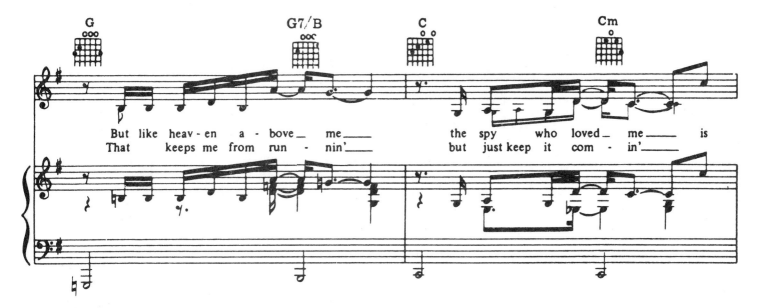

But like heav-en a-bove__ me__ the spy who loved__ me__ is
That keeps me from run - nin'__ but just keep it com - in'__

keep-in' all my se-crets safe to - night.
how'd you learn to do the things you do? And

No - bod - y does ___ it bet - ter _____ makes me feel sad _____ for the

rest. No - bod - y does _ it _____ half as good as you.

Ba - by, ba - by, ba - by you're the best.

RIGHT TIME OF THE NIGHT

Words and Music by
PETER McCANN

Right Time of the Night - 3 - 3

LET'S MAKE LOVE

Words and Music by
MARV GREEN, CHRIS LINDSEY,
BILL LUTHER and AIMEE MAYO

Moderately slow ♩ = 72

Let's Make Love - 6 - 1

IF WALLS COULD TALK

Words and Music by
R. J. LANGE

If Walls Could Talk - 7 - 1

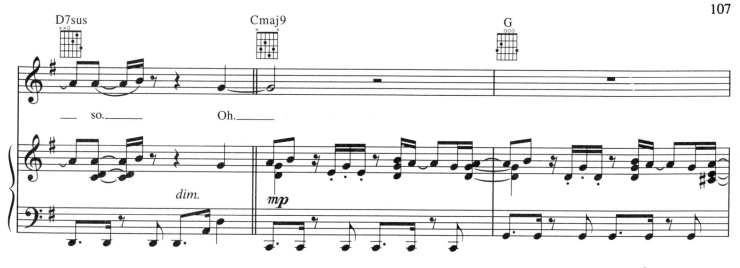

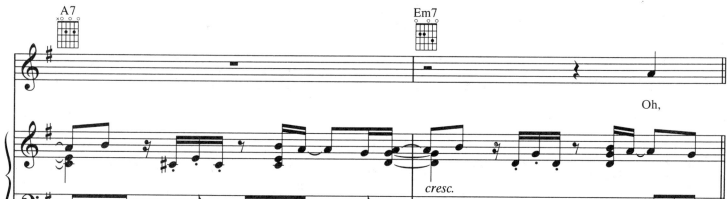

hear no vi - o - lins,_____ you play___ my ev - 'ry string._____ So

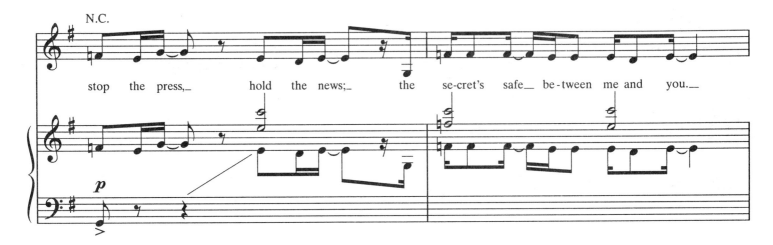

stop the press,_ hold the news;_ the se-cret's safe_ be-tween me and you._

Walls,_____ can you keep a se - cret?_____ If walls_ could

Chorus:

talk, oh, they would say, "I want_ you more."_ They would say, "Hey, nev-er

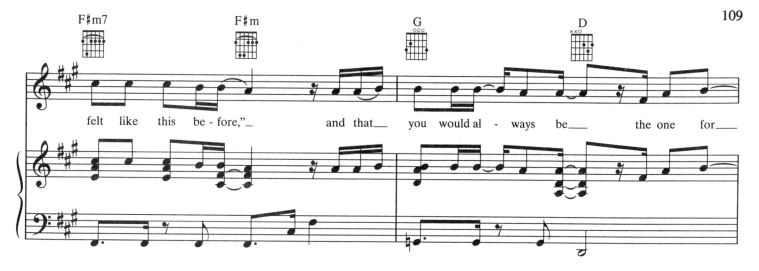

felt like this be-fore,"_ and that_ you would al - ways be_ the one for_

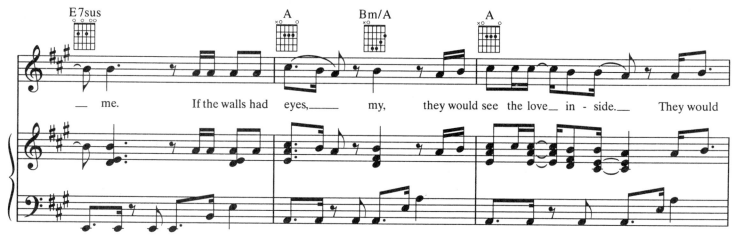

_ me. If the walls had eyes,_ my, they would see the love_ in - side._ They would

see me in your arms in ec - sta - sy._ And with_

ev - 'ry move,_they'd know_ I love you_ so._____ *I love you so.*

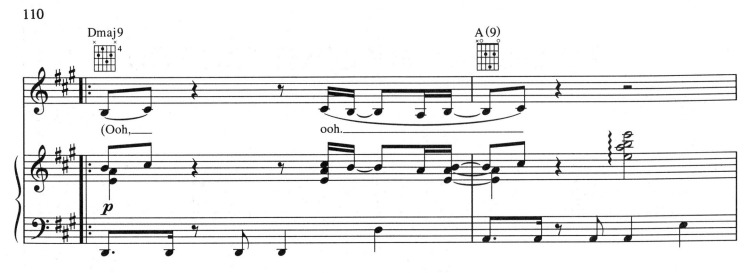

Repeat ad lib. and fade

SAVING ALL MY LOVE FOR YOU

Words by
GERRY GOFFIN

Music by
MICHAEL MASSER

Slowly

A few stolen mo-ments is all that we share.
not ver-y eas-y liv-ing all a-lone. My

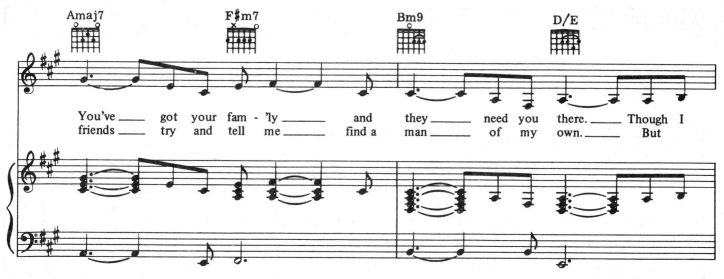

You've got your fam-'ly and they need you there. Though I
friends try and tell me find a man of my own. But

Saving All My Love for You - 5 - 1

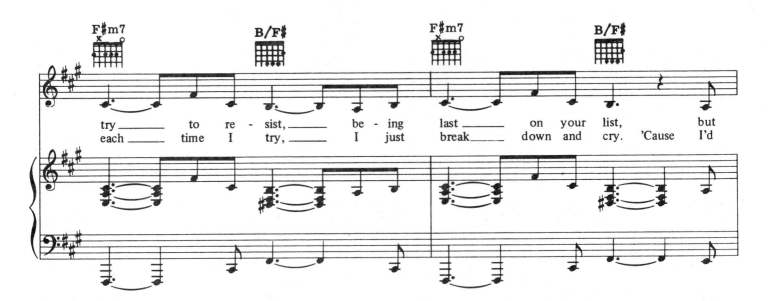

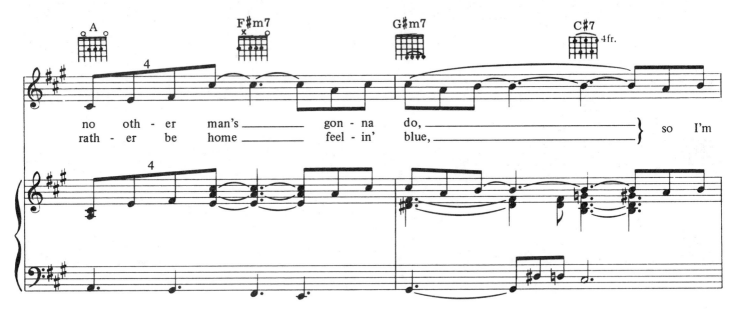

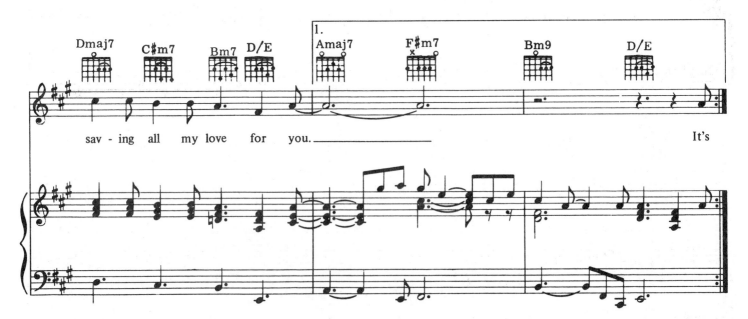

POWER OF LOVE/LOVE POWER

Words and Music by LUTHER VANDROSS
and MARCUS MILLER

Words and Music by TEDDY VANN

LOVE POWER

pow-er __ of love. _____

When __ we walk __ down the street, we __ don't

care who __ we see _____ or who __ we meet. _____ Don't need to run, _

_____ don't need to hide _____ 'cause we've got

SET THE NIGHT TO MUSIC

Words and Music by
DIANE WARREN

124

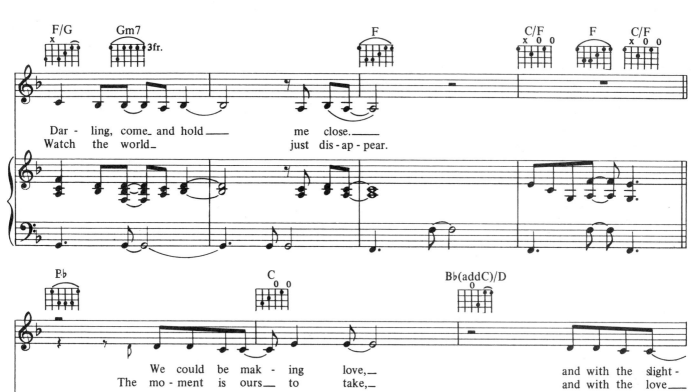

126

The mo - ment is ours to take,_____

Set the Night to Music - 6 - 5

and with the love____ we make,____   and with the slight -

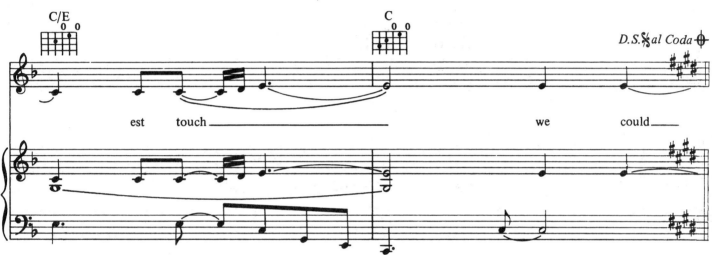

est touch _____ we could____

____ ic._____   Set the night,____
ic.)

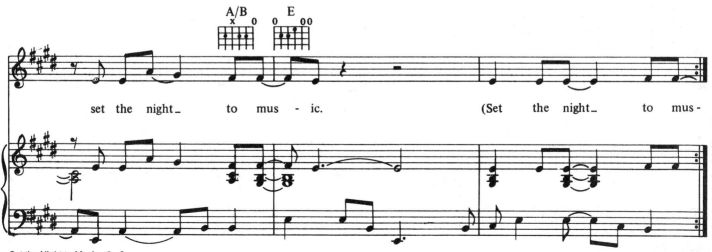

set the night_ to mus - ic.   (Set the night_ to mus -

SLOW HAND

Words and Music by
MICHAEL CLARK and JOHN BETTIS

Slow Hand - 4 - 1

HAVE I TOLD YOU LATELY

Words and Music by
VAN MORRISON

Slowly, with expression

Have I told ___ you late-ly that I love you? Have I

told you there's no one else ___ a-bove ___ you?

Fill my heart ___ with glad - ness, take a-way all ___ my sad - ness,

TRULY

Words and Music by
LIONEL RICHIE

THEN CAME YOU

Words and Music by
PHIL PUGH and SHERMAN MARSHALL

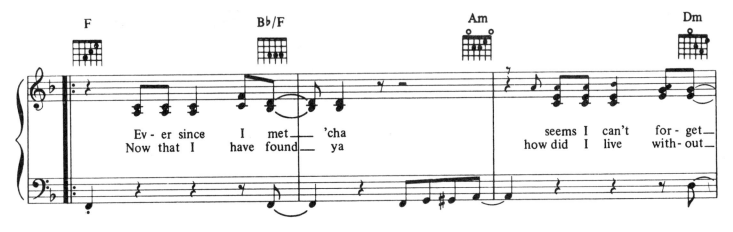

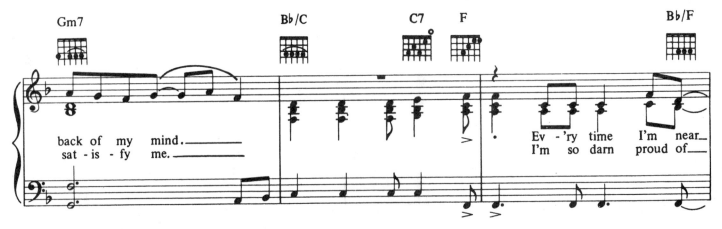

Then Came You - 4 - 1

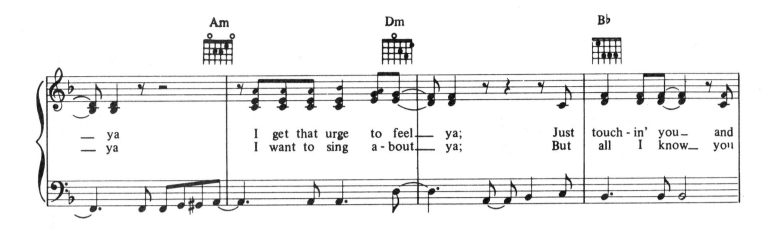

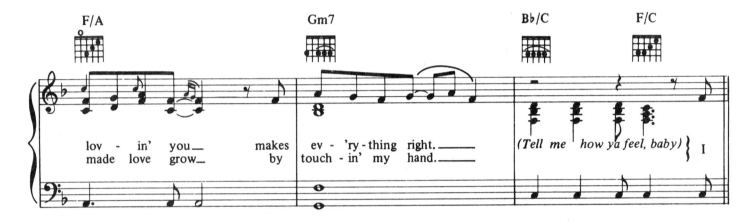

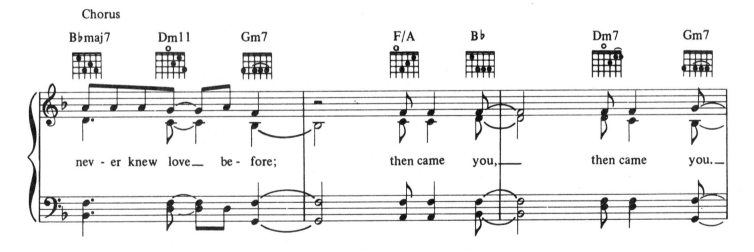

Then Came You - 4 - 2

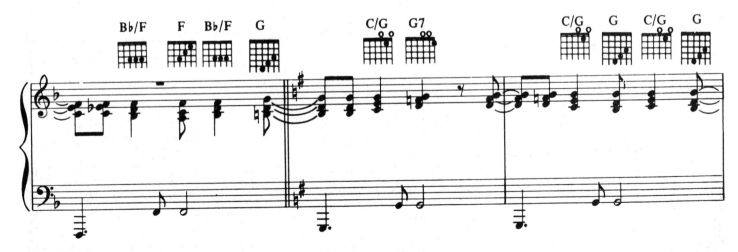

TONIGHT I CELEBRATE MY LOVE

Words and Music by
MICHAEL MASSER and GERRY GOFFIN

Verse 3:
Tonight I celebrate my love for you,
And soon this old world will seem brand new.
Tonight we will both discover
How friends turn into lovers,
When I make love to you.
(To Chorus:)

THE WAY I WANT TO TOUCH YOU

Words and Music by
TONI TENNILLE

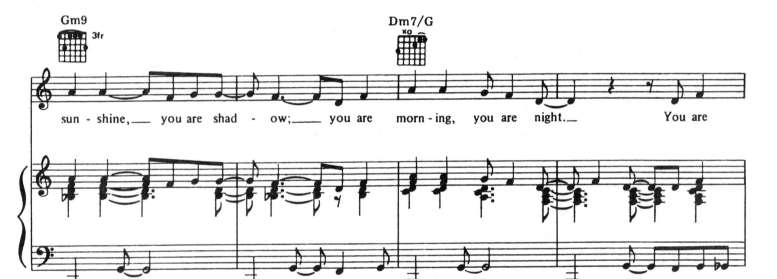

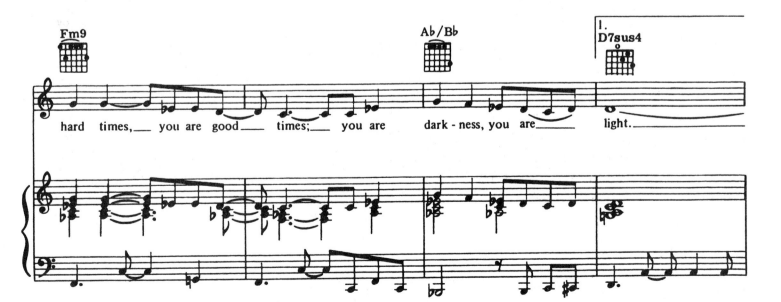

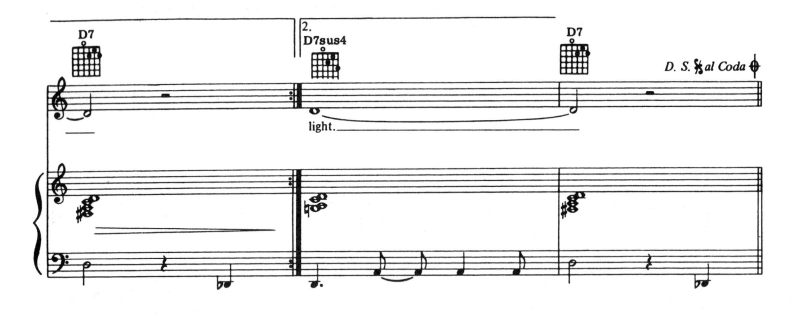

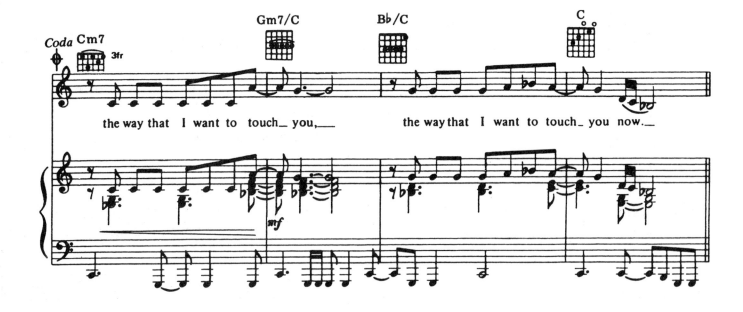

(Slow Dancin') SWAYIN' TO THE MUSIC

Words and Music by
JACK TEMPCHIN

Swayin' to the Music - 3 - 1

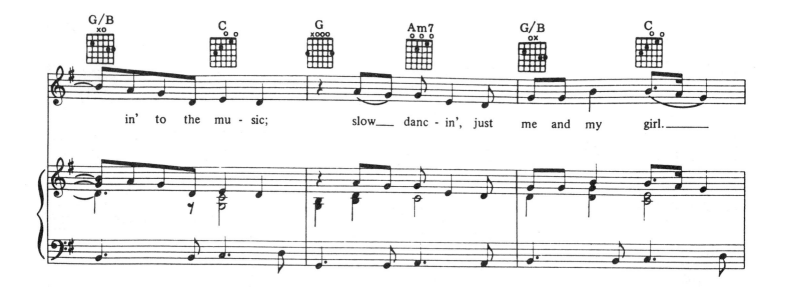

in' to the mu - sic; slow___ danc - in', just me and my girl.___

Slow___ danc - in', sway - in' to the mu - sic. No one else___ in the

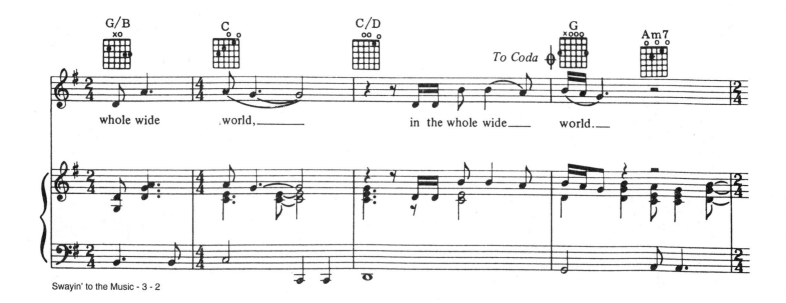

whole wide ___world,___ in the whole wide___ world.___

YOU GIVE GOOD LOVE

Words and Music by
LA FORREST "LA LA" COPE

Moderately, with a beat ♩ = 76

Verse 1:

1. I found out what I've been miss - ing al - ways on the run.

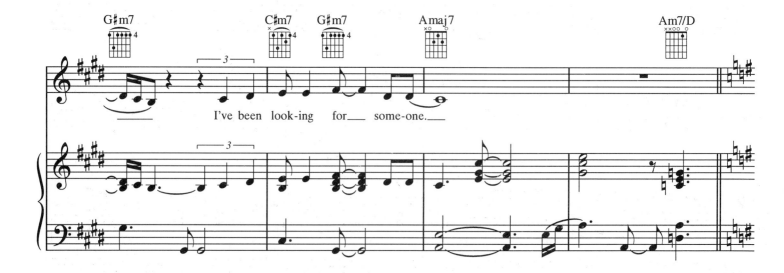

I've been look-ing for some-one.

Verse 2:

Ba - by, you give good love.____

2. Nev - er stop - ping,__ I was al - ways search - ing____ for that per - fect love,__

the kind that girls like me____ dream of._____

Now you're here____ like you've been____ be - fore,__ and you know____ just what__ I need.__

YOU'LL NEVER FIND
ANOTHER LOVE LIKE MINE

Words and Music by
KENNETH GAMBLE and LEON HUFF

Moderately

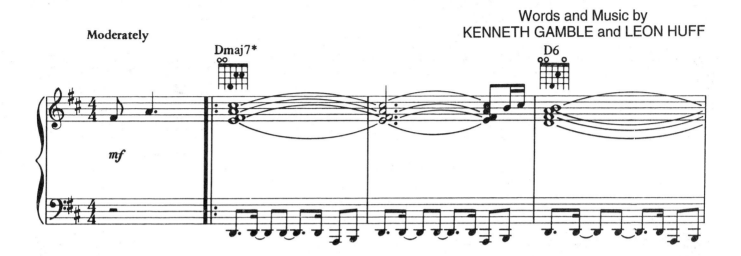

You'll nev-er find,_____
You'll nev-er find,_____
You'll nev-er find,_____

It-'ll take the

as long as you live,_____
end of all time,_____
an-other love like mine

*Guitarists: Tune lowest string to D

You'll Never Find Another Love Like Mine - 5 - 1

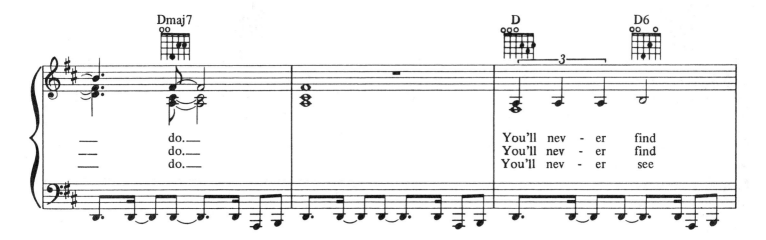

You'll Never Find Another Love Like Mine - 5 - 2

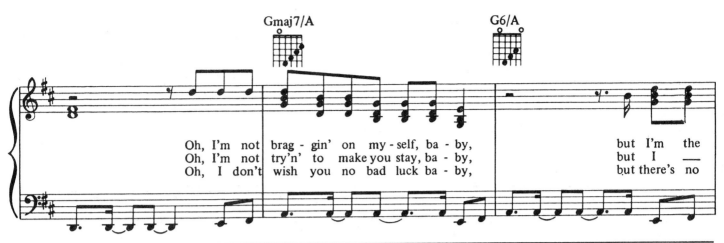

Oh, I'm not brag - gin' on my - self, ba - by,
Oh, I'm not try'n' to make you stay, ba - by,
Oh, I don't wish you no bad luck ba - by,

but I'm the
but I —
but there's no

one who loves you, and there's no one else, no

one else.

know some - how— some - day— some way:—
may - be's —

You're gon - na miss my lov - in'

(Late in the mid-night hour, ba-by____) You're gon - na miss my lov-in'When it's

cold out-side____ You're gon - na miss my lov-in'

(miss, you're gon-na miss my love.____)

D   Dmaj7   D6

Gmaj7/A

D.S. and fade on chorus

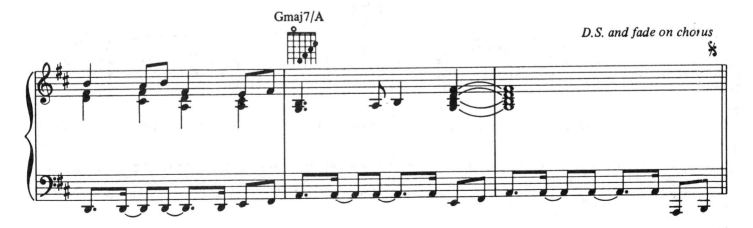

You'll Never Find Another Love Like Mine - 5 - 5

YOU MAKE ME FEEL BRAND NEW

Words and Music by
THOM BELL and LINDA CREED

Slow and pretty

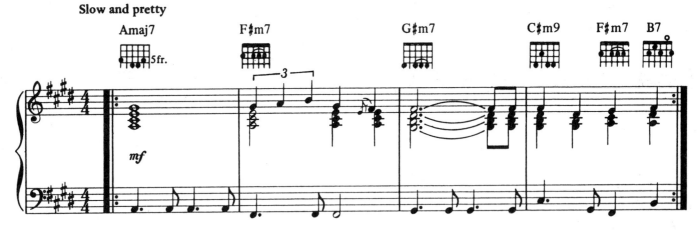

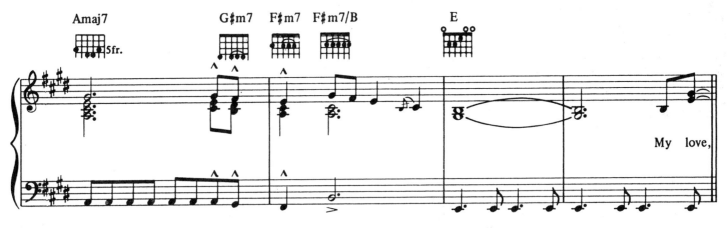

My love,

I'll nev- er find the words, my love, To
when- ev- er I was in - se - cure, You

tell you how I feel, my love.
built me up and made me sure.

Mere words You gave
could not my pride

You Make Me Feel Brand New - 4 - 1

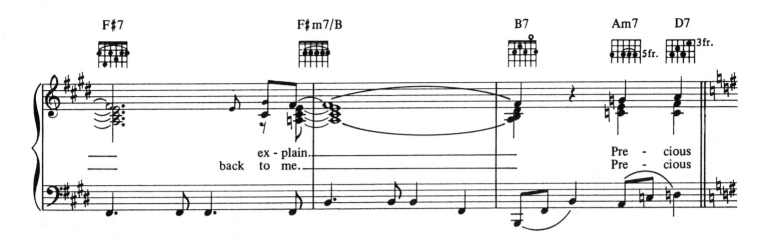

You Make Me Feel Brand New - 4 - 2

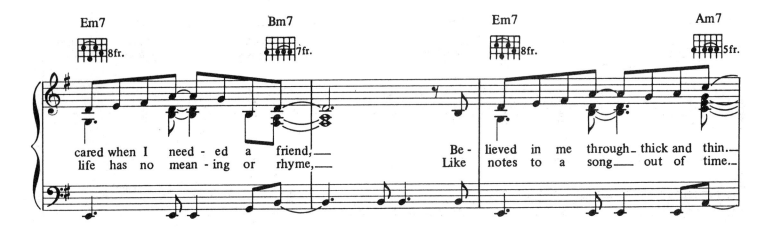

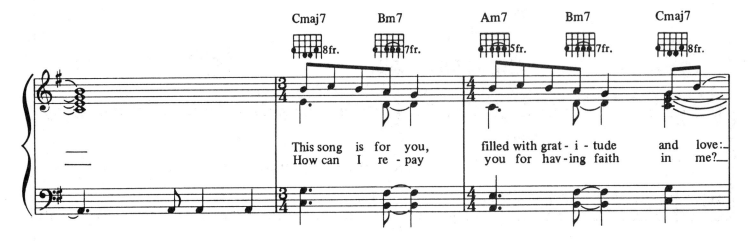

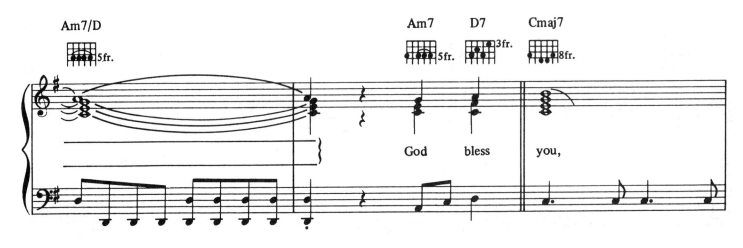

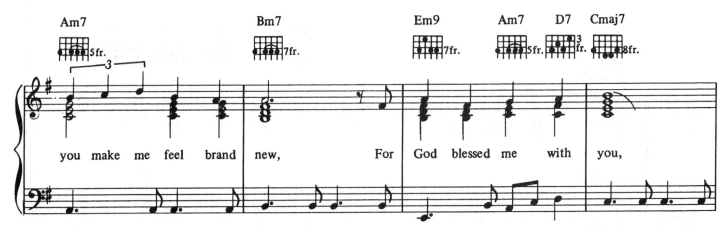

you make me feel brand new, I sing this song 'cause for

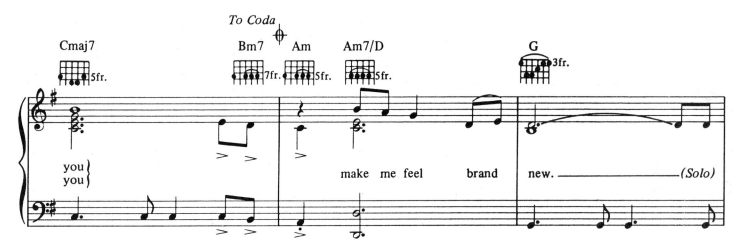

To Coda

you / you make me feel brand new. _____ (Solo)

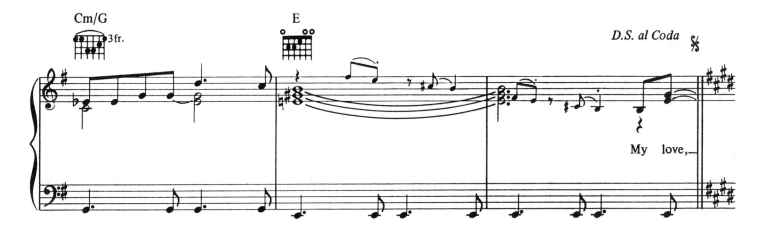

D.S. al Coda

My love,

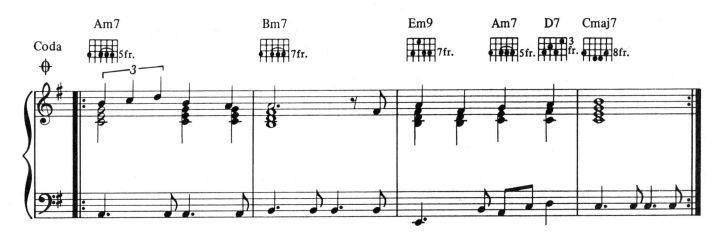

Coda

LET'S MAKE A NIGHT TO REMEMBER

Words and Music by
BRYAN ADAMS and ROBERT JOHN "MUTT" LANGE

Verse:

1. I love the way ya look to - night,

with your hair hang - in' down on your shoul - ders._

'N' I love the way ya dance your slow, sweet tan - go,

the way ya wan - na do ev-

Let's Make a Night To Remember - 8 - 1

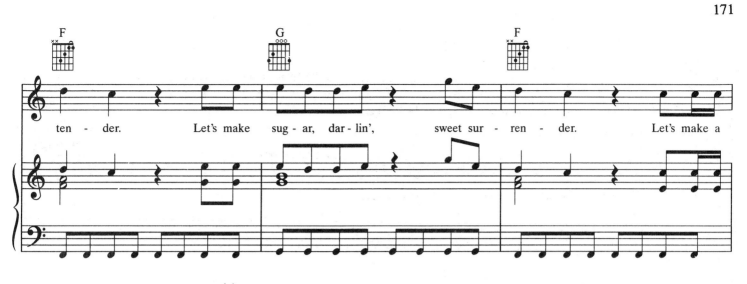

ten - der. Let's make sug - ar, dar - lin', sweet sur - ren - der. Let's make a

To Coda

night to re - mem - ber all life long.

Verse:

2. I love the way ya move___ to - night, beads___ of sweat drip - pin' down___

cem - ber. Let's make love___ to ex - cite us, a mem - o -

ry___ to ig - nite us. Let's make hon - ey, ba - by, soft and

ten - der. Let's make sug - ar, dar - lin', sweet sur - ren - der. Let's make a

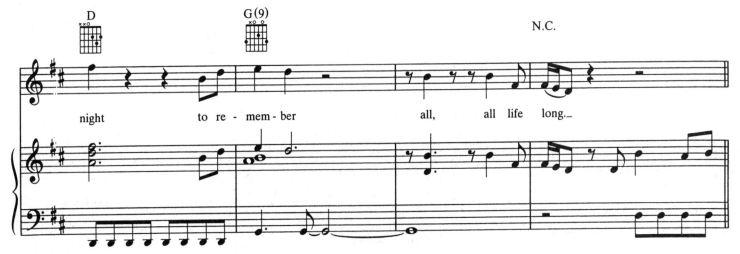

night to re - mem - ber all, all life long.___

INSEPARABLE

Words and Music by
CHARLES JACKSON and
MARVIN JEROME YANCY

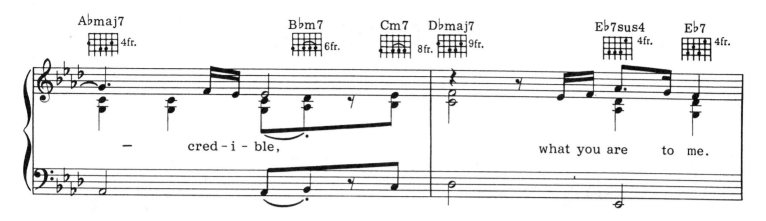

—cred-i-ble, what you are to me.

In-cred-i-ble, you bring out the wom-an in__ me

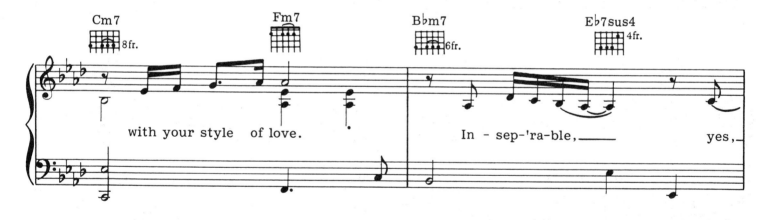

with your style of love. In-sep-'ra-ble,____ yes,—

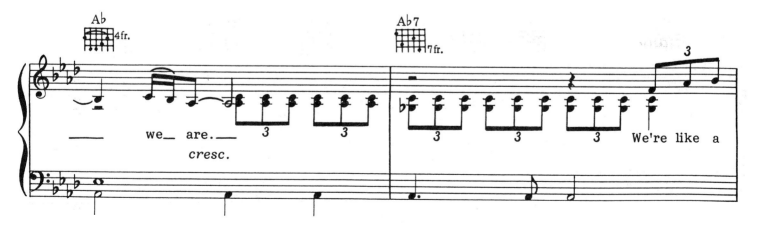

—__ we__ are.__ *cresc.* We're like a

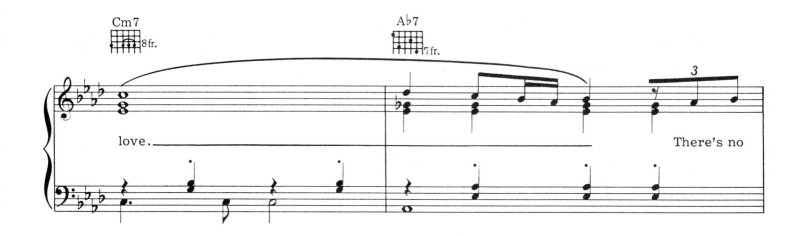

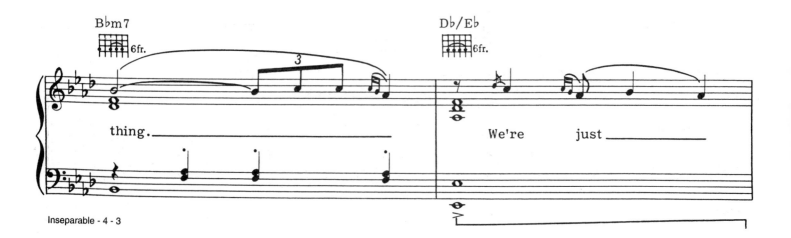

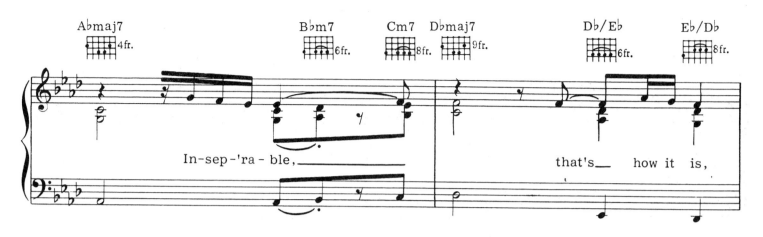

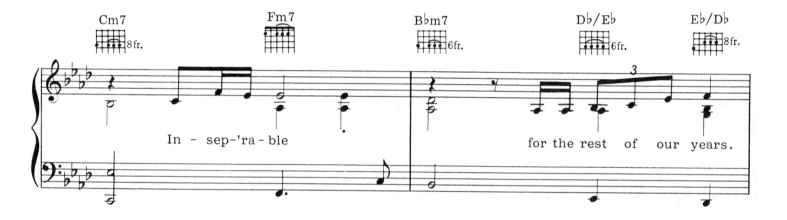

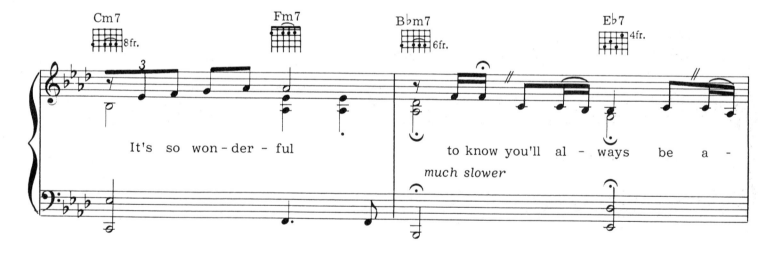

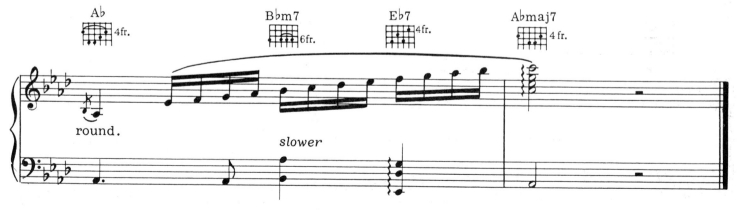

Inseparable - 4 - 4

WHEN A MAN LOVES A WOMAN

Words and Music by
CALVIN LEWIS and ANDREW WRIGHT

Easy feel, in 2

When a man___ loves a wom - an, can't keep his mind on noth - in' else.
man___ loves a wom - an, spend his ver - y last dime

He'd trade the world for a good thing he's found. If she is bad,___ he can't
try - ing to hold on to what he needs. He'd give up all___ his

When a Man Loves a Woman - 4 - 1

MY FIRST NIGHT WITH YOU

Words and Music by
DIANE WARREN and BABYFACE

My First Night With You - 5 - 1

true _____

my first night ____ with you.

my first night ____ with you.

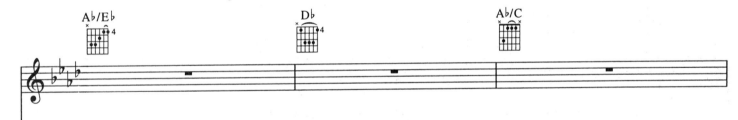

D.S.%al Coda

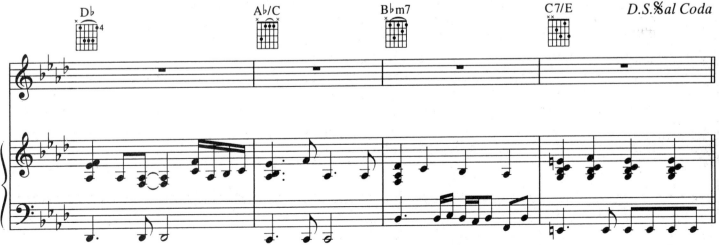